Baby Farm Animals

I0878130

Baby Sheep

By Nick Rebman

level 1

little blue readers

www.littlebluehousebooks.com

Little Blue House is distributed by North Star Editions:
sales@northstareditions.com | 888-417-0195

Produced for Little Blue House by Red Line Editorial.

Photographs ©: Shutterstock Images, cover, 4, 7, 9, 11, 13, 14, 17, 18–19, 20, 23, 24 (top left), 24 (top right), 24 (bottom left), 24 (bottom right)

Library of Congress Control Number: 2021916733

ISBN
978-1-64619-479-7 (hardcover)
978-1-64619-506-0 (paperback)
978-1-64619-559-6 (ebook pdf)
978-1-64619-533-6 (hosted ebook)

Printed in the United States of America
Mankato, MN
012022

About the Author

Nick Rebman is a writer and editor who lives in Minnesota. He enjoys reading, drawing, and taking long walks with his dog.

Table of Contents

mother

Baby Sheep

A baby sheep is born.

Its mother licks it clean.

Soon the baby sheep
can stand.
It walks on the straw.

straw

The baby sheep
goes outside.
It stays near its mother.

The baby sheep has
big ears.
It also has soft hair.
Its hair is called wool.

ear
wool

The baby sheep likes to play.
It plays with another baby sheep.

Eating and Drinking

The baby sheep drinks milk.

It gets milk from its mother.

Soon the baby sheep eats food.
It eats grass and other plants.

grass

The baby sheep

drinks water.

The water is in a tub.

water

Growing Up

Sometimes it gets cold outside. The baby sheep can go into a barn.

The baby sheep starts to grow up.

It gets bigger and bigger.

Glossary

barn

milk

grass

straw

Index